Harvesting Medicine on the Hill

by Joyce Guttmacher
illustrated by Kate McKeon

PEARSON

Scott Foresman

Editorial Offices: Glenview, Illinois • Parsippany, New Jersey • New York, New York
Sales Offices: Needham, Massachusetts • Duluth, Georgia • Glenview, Illinois
Coppell, Texas • Ontario, California • Mesa, Arizona

    Picture yourself in a pharmacy, standing in front of the shelves of medicines. Rows and rows of perfectly shaped pills in white sterile bottles, topped off with balls of cotton and tamper-proof caps, stand at attention. Now turn around, and imagine time slipping backwards, backwards, backwards. The flickering fluorescent lights fade, the walls of the store dissolve away, and you are—where?

It is a long, long time ago in the 1500s, and you are standing alone on the crest of a hill that overlooks the wild California coast. Gnarled oaks spot the golden yellow hills beneath you, all the way down to where the ocean crashes against the shore. The pharmacy is gone and all the medicines in it—or are they?

Surprising as it might seem, the slopes of these sun-baked hills *are* a kind of pharmacy. The brush, bushes, wildflowers, and weeds have all been used for thousands of years to cure and prevent illness.

As you look over this hill of wildly flowering medicines, you see an old man hobbling up the steep side of the hill. Somehow, you know him. His name is

Bent Oak Kitsepawit, and he is a Chumash elder. You also recognize his grandson, Red Hawk, following at a respectful distance. The bit of root around his neck bounces on his collarbone as he scrambles up the slopes.

"Are we almost there?" he calls out to Bent Oak.

"If I remember correctly," the old man replies. "I saw some *chuchupate* growing by the marshy place near the stream, back last spring."

"Why didn't you pick it in the spring, then?" the boy asks innocently.

"Remember, my child," Bent Oak answers evenly, "we do not pick chuchupate in the spring. We pick it in fall, when all the power is in the roots."

Bent Oak squats beside another plant and asks, "Do you recall what *yerba mansa* is used for?"

Red Hawk is still learning—it has only been a year now that he has been accompanying his grandfather to the hills. "Yerba mansa cures burning pains under the skin," he recites slowly and carefully.

"That's right, my child," Bent Oak replies. "Put yerba mansa on wounds and they will heal. Drink it as tea to purify the blood. We will pull up the roots now, bring them back to the *'ap*, and dry them. In a few weeks, we can slice them and begin to use them for medicine."

As Bent Oak stands and looks toward the coast, he frowns at a building, much larger than the 'ap where he and the boy live, that is under construction.

"What are they doing, Grandfather?" the boy asks about the foreigners who are working on the strange-looking building.

"They are cutting down too many of our oak trees," Bent Oak says curtly. "That takes too many trees that give food."

Red Hawk nods. Though most of the food in the village comes from the sea, they eat bread from the *chia*, or acorns—the seeds of the oak tree—every day.

Red Hawk looks back to where the workers labor on the building for the Spanish strangers. He can see them breaking up the earth to plant seeds. *What will their arrival mean to our people?* he wonders.

A Spanish mission

Chuchupate

"We should not stand here idly," says the grandfather, turning his back on the new building. "We have many more medicinal plants to find." The urgency in Bent Oak's voice makes the boy uneasy. He thinks about the rumors he has heard at night in the 'ap, about the sickness in the south, where people break out in rashes of oozing red sores. They said the sick went blind or died. Red Hawk worries that the sickness will reach his village too. For weeks, he has been afraid to ask his grandfather whether the sickness will continue its deadly trek up north.

Casting a last nervous look behind him, Red Hawk asks, "What else do we need?" trying to hide his fear.

The old man touches his hand to the bit of twisted root he wears on a cord around his neck. It is an answer, and the boy understands. "Chuchupate," Bent Oak smiles. "And do you remember why it is important?"

"It guards against rattlesnakes," the boy answers promptly. "Grandmother chews the root for headaches. Uncle rubs it on his sore body after fishing, and mother gives me chuchupate tea when I am sick with a cold."

The grandfather nods. "Yes, chuchupate has many uses. You can see how important it is that we bring more home to the village. Come up the hill to where it grows. You should know by now where to find it."

"Grandfather," the boy pants, scrambling after the old medicine man, "if the chuchupate is so important, why don't we plant it near the village?"

"Chuchupate does not consent to be grown just anywhere," Bent Oak answers. "Some plants can be cultivated, but chuchupate only grows where it wants. Do you remember why we must be careful when we pick chuchupate?"

Red Hawk says slowly and thoughtfully, "It is because we take the root. If we only took the flower, the plant would still be there next year. But because we take the root, there will be no plants left at all if we take too much."

His grandfather nods. "That is why," Bent Oak says, "and that is what the strangers do not understand. I do not want to tell them about the chuchupate."

"Don't they know about it?" the boy asks curiously. The old man shakes his head. The boy is amazed. "And is it true that they have no doctors— no pipe doctors, or ant doctors, or herb doctors?"

Ruda, a medicinal herb

Poison oak

Bent Oak speaks as they walk, "I don't believe they have doctors like our doctors, and I've heard they look down on our pipe doctors and other shaman. They have their own cures and their own plants. Some say that the plant called *rue* is good for earache. It grows in their gardens. But they do not know our remedies and perhaps should not try to use them."

The boy thinks about the pipe doctors who suck out whatever is causing disease through their long stone pipes. Thinking of sickness reminds him of the sick people in the south. He does not want to think about that; instead, he asks Bent Oak why the Spanish don't use their medicines.

"Well, Red Hawk, think of this. Do you remember what should be used for warts and rashes on the skin?"

"You must use the juice of the poison oak when it is cut in the spring," Red Hawk recites from memory.

The old man nods. "The poison oak plant is important because it is a cure and a poison. It can cure stomach upset if you boil it and drink it when cool, but you must keep the smoke out of your eyes, or it could blind you." The boy nods, for he remembers boiling it last summer.

"Why did you say the Spanish should not use it?"

"When they touch the plant," Bent Oak replies, "they break out in a terrible rash. It is very strange, that one people should be affected by it when another is not, but perhaps there is a reason." Seeing Red Hawk's discomfort, Bent Oak asks gently, "If *you* had a rash, what could you do for it?"

"Mugwort," the boy answers quickly. "I would make a tea of mugwort leaves, and use it to bathe the rash."

Mugwort

Owl's clover

Coyote tobacco

The old man nods proudly. "You remember well. What else is the mugwort used for?"

"You make the dried leaves into a little cone. Then you put it on a wound to keep it from becoming infected," answers Red Hawk.

"Yes," the grandfather nods. "That is right." Bent Oak strides across the hill with the boy following behind. Beautiful twisted oaks make patterns against the yellow grass and the blue sky. The relentless autumn sun releases the rich smell of the grass, and the boy breathes deeply. The old man listens to the sawing drone of the insects and admires the sudden flight of the birds that nested there. It is the way it has always been.

Red Hawk, however, worries and squeezes his eyes shut. He wants to hear his grandfather assure him that there are plants that will cure the sickness brought to the people in the south by the strangers who have invaded their land. He wants his grandfather to say that the pipe doctors will be able to suck it away.

But Red Hawk's grandfather says nothing. He merely walks on, unhurried, planting one foot in front of the other as if there is no terrible sickness to the south.

The boy follows behind, trying to mimic his grandfather's easy gait, hoping it will quell the worry in his own heart. Then his grandfather stops and squats beside a tall hairy-stemmed plant that stands among the grasses, its bell-shaped flowers still blooming, even in September.

"Coyote tobacco," the boy volunteers, without being asked. "Its smoke is used by the pipe doctors."

"That's right," the old man smiles. "The pipe doctor blows its smoke over the sick, so that they will get better. Do you remember other uses for coyote tobacco?"

"We drink it for stomach pains," the boy says, "and also rub it where the body hurts. I had it on

my ears before they were pierced so they would not hurt too much."

Bent Oak nods, "Yes, it is good for you to remember these things, for someday it may be you who teach others."

It was strange. Last year, before the Spanish came and the sickness came, the boy loved to hear his grandfather's praise. He loved hearing that someday it would be he who would know the healing powers of plants.

But today, his grandfather's words sound ominous. Red Hawk fears that if the sickness comes and takes his grandfather, he will not remember when to harvest the chuchupate and how to prepare the coyote tobacco. Perhaps no one else will know.

Will our doctors protect us? Red Hawk wants to ask. The question leaves a bitter taste in his mouth. He does not want to ask it, however, and—as if from a distance—he hears his grandfather say that the doctors can do little.

When the strange building reappears over the rise, he cannot help but ask, "Grandfather, will the doctors be able to protect us if the southern sickness comes here?"

His grandfather stops walking, turns, and stands stock-still facing the boy. Looking as if words have escaped from him, he gives his answer slowly, deliberately. "I do not know."

The boy closes his eyes. There is sadness in his grandfather's voice such as he has never heard before. Red Hawk knows that his grandfather, too, is worried about the sickness that follows the Spanish. When he opens his eyes again, his grandfather is gazing at him gently.

"There is one plant we have not discussed today, my child. Perhaps it will help us. Do you know which plant I am talking about?"

The boy does. It is *toloache*, the jimsonweed, and it is very dangerous—too much toloache causes blindness, insanity, and death. Taken in moderation, toloache is also a powerful way to strengthen the body and protect it. The boy knows that people take it to clean the blood or dull the worst pain.

Toloache is so potent that it needs to be prepared in a special way. It must be done by a relative, preferably the mother or grandmother of the person who is to take it. It must never be done lightly. The boy wonders if he should take toloache to ward off the unknown sickness if it comes to his village.

They go together over the fields, searching, until they come to a tall plant with enormous white flowers like trumpets—a bushy plant that comes up to the boy's middle.

"You must be careful," his grandfather says, holding the boy back as he reaches to grasp the plant. "Toloache is dangerous. It can even hurt the skin." The boy watches how the old man harvests the plant carefully.

"Will the toloache save us?" the boy asks.

"My son, it is not the plants that cure us, you know that. Sickness comes from imbalance and must be cured by restoring balance. The pipe doctor can suck out whatever it is that is making us sick. The power of the plants is in how they are used—how the mother prepares the toloache, how the pipe doctor blows his smoke over the patient. That is what you must remember."

Toloache

The village is bustling when the boy and his grandfather return to the 'ap with their collection of plants. Several women sit outside in the dusk, weaving baskets, while two girls dye more rushes to be used in making baskets. The boy spies his own mother, crouching beside a fire. A large basket is on the ground beside her. His mother's baskets are so tightly woven that they can hold water. Now she heats up rocks in the fire—when they are hot enough she will put them into the acorn gruel in the basket and cook it for supper.

A few men come up the path from the sea, carrying the day's catch of fish. Some boys play with walnut shell dice in the dirt, while others throw a sharp pole through a circle of willow. In the distance, the steam rises from the 'apa'yik, or sweathouse, where the men sit to cleanse and purify themselves and talk about the day's events.

The boy looks up to where the sun carries its torch of burning bark across the sky. Soon it will sink in the west, sending a shower of sparks across the sky to shine in the dark and give comfort in the night.

He remembers what his grandfather always says: other people must struggle to live, but his people have all that they want for the taking. Instead of working in the dirt, they have time to play games, to weave beautiful baskets, to carve the *tomol* canoes that carry them over the sea to the islands. Red Hawk vows he will do everything in his power to help preserve his people and their way of life.

Medicines from Nature

All over the world, in all times and places, human beings have used plants to treat illness and injury. Plants with antibacterial or antifungal properties (like yerba mansa, goldenseal, and others) have been used over the years to:

- treat infections
- slow down or speed up respiration and heart rate
- kill pain, bring down fever, aid breathing
- treat warts and rashes
- bring on or delay childbirth

Although there are not enough experiments to measure the effectiveness of herbal remedies, the chemical composition of many plants has been shown to have measurable effects on the human body. Moreover, several plants are the basis for modern medicines:

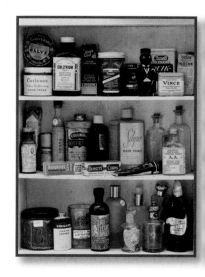

- The foxglove plant is used in the heart drug digitalis.
- Poppy seeds are used in the pain medication morphine.
- The mayapple is used in the wart medicine podophyllum.

One of the most common drugs of all comes from the willow. Native Americans have long boiled down this plant to make a tea to bring down fever and dull pain. Today, people buy that cure in a drugstore and call it aspirin.